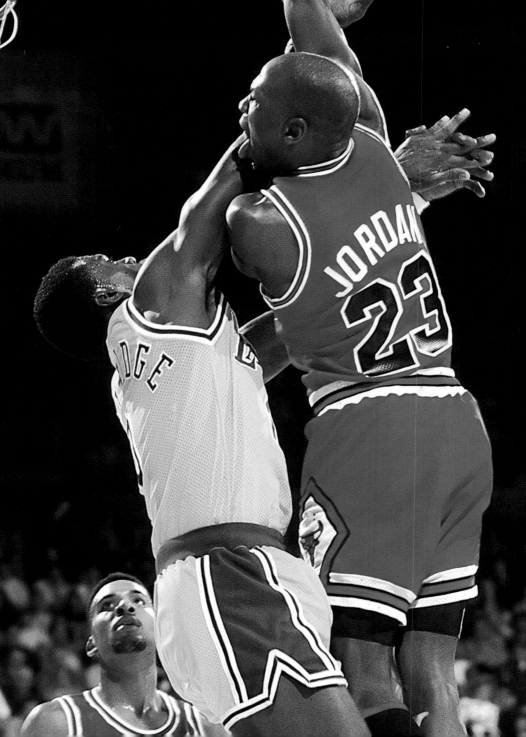

ILLINOIS

ILLINOIS
Valerie Bodden

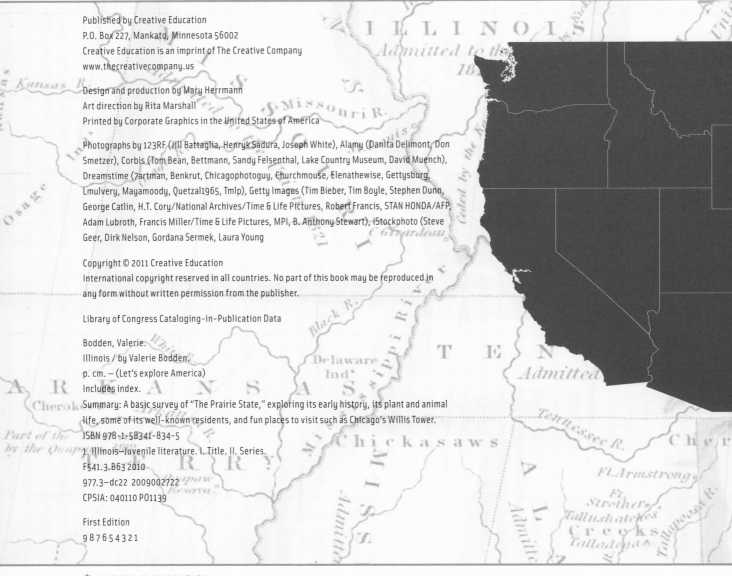

Published by Creative Education
P.O. Box 227, Mankato, Minnesota 56002
Creative Education is an imprint of The Creative Company
www.thecreativecompany.us

Design and production by Mary Herrmann
Art direction by Rita Marshall
Printed by Corporate Graphics in the United States of America

Photographs by 123RF (Jill Battaglia, Henryk Sadura, Joseph White), Alamy (Danita Delimont, Don Smetzer), Corbis (Tom Bean, Bettmann, Sandy Felsenthal, Lake Country Museum, David Muench), Dreamstime (7artman, Benkrut, Chicagophotoguy, Churchmouse, Elenathewise, Gettysburg, Lmulvery, Mayamoody, Quetzal1965, Tmlp), Getty Images (Tim Bieber, Tim Boyle, Stephen Dunn, George Catlin, H.T. Cory/National Archives/Time & Life Pictures, Robert Francis, STAN HONDA/AFP, Adam Lubroth, Francis Miller/Time & Life Pictures, MPI, B. Anthony Stewart), iStockphoto (Steve Geer, Dirk Nelson, Gordana Sermek, Laura Young)

Library of Congress Cataloging-in-Publication Data

Bodden, Valerie.
Illinois / by Valerie Bodden.
p. cm. – (Let's explore America)
Includes index.
Summary: A basic survey of "The Prairie State," exploring its early history, its plant and animal life, some of its well-known residents, and fun places to visit such as Chicago's Willis Tower.
ISBN 978-1-58341-834-5
1. Illinois–Juvenile literature. I. Title. II. Series.
F541.3.B63 2010
977.3–dc22   2009002722
CPSIA: 040110 PO1139

First Edition
9 8 7 6 5 4 3 2 1

Illinois is a state in the middle part of America. It is a medium-sized state. Illinois became a state in 1818. Illinois is nicknamed "The **Prairie** State." This is because it was once covered by prairies.

TOP, THEN LEFT TO RIGHT:
- The Illinois prairie
- An old map showing Illinois and other states
- African Americans moving to Illinois in the late 1800s
- The log cabin that Abraham Lincoln lived in as a boy
- A worker in an Illinois coal mine

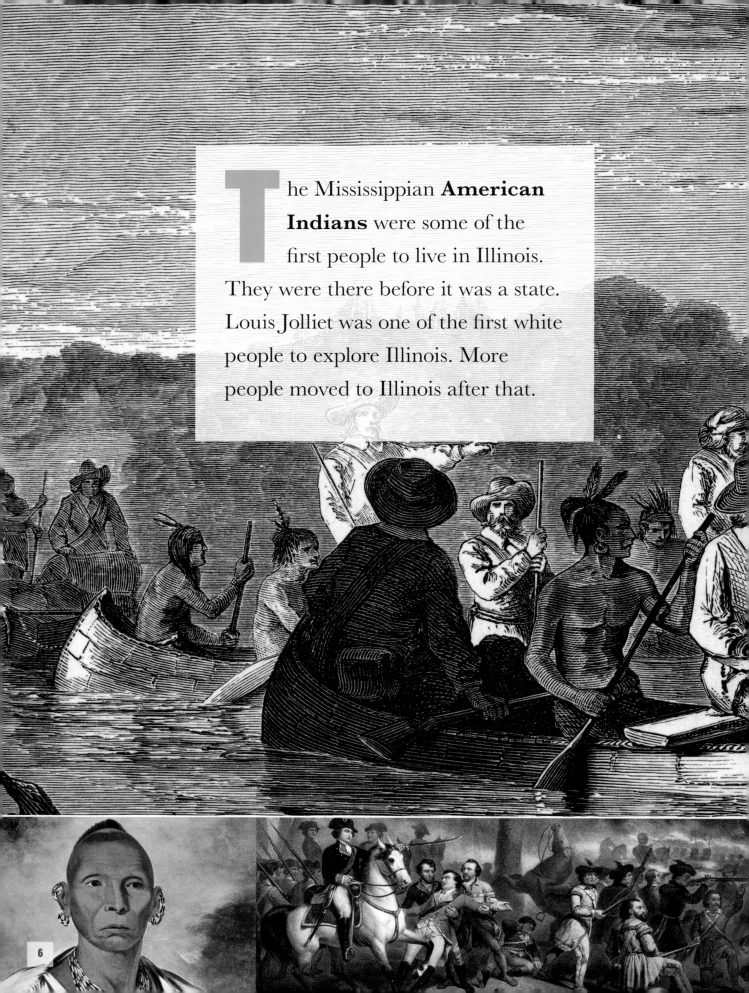

The Mississippian **American Indians** were some of the first people to live in Illinois. They were there before it was a state. Louis Jolliet was one of the first white people to explore Illinois. More people moved to Illinois after that.

TOP, THEN LEFT TO RIGHT:
- *Illinois Indians helping to guide explorer Louis Jolliet*
- *An Illinois Indian leader named Black Hawk*
- *A scene from a war in the 1700s to control Illinois and the land around it*
- *People in Illinois wearing clothes from their home country of Poland*
- *A boat carrying people to Illinois*

TOP, THEN LEFT TO RIGHT:

- *A bridge over the Illinois River in Peoria, Illinois*
- *The Fox River running through Illinois*
- *Lake Michigan and the city of Chicago in the winter*
- *An Illinois field in the summer*

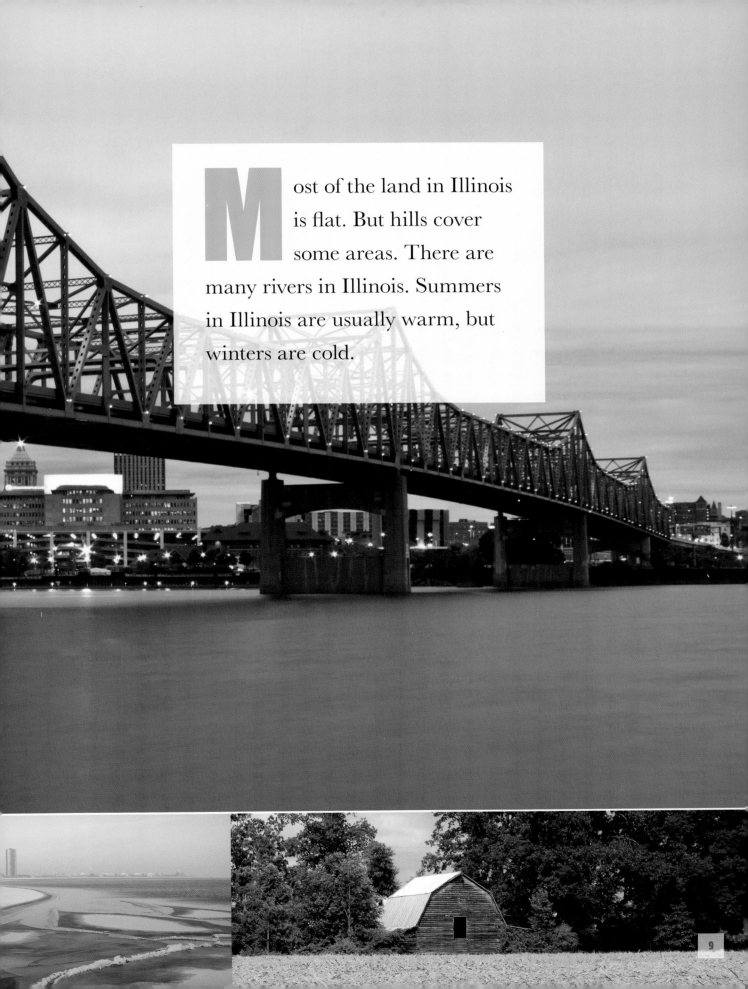

Most of the land in Illinois is flat. But hills cover some areas. There are many rivers in Illinois. Summers in Illinois are usually warm, but winters are cold.

Farmers in Illinois grow soybeans, corn, and wheat. Forests of oak and hickory trees grow in some parts of Illinois. Deer and turkeys live in the forests.

TOP, THEN LEFT TO RIGHT:

• *An Illinois farm*
• *An Illinois farmer using horses to pull a farm wagon*
• *Wild turkeys*
• *Soybean plants*
• *Deer in an Illinois forest*

Illinois' state flower is the violet. The violet is a small flower that can be purple, blue, white, or yellow. Illinois' state bird is the cardinal. The cardinal is a small, red bird. Illinois' state tree is the white oak. The white oak is a big tree with gray-white bark.

TOP, THEN LEFT TO RIGHT:

- *A cardinal*
- *The leaves of an oak tree in the fall*
- *Purple violets*
- *White oak trees in the spring*

TOP, THEN LEFT TO RIGHT:

- *Cows on an Illinois dairy farm*
- *President Abraham Lincoln (at center)*
- *Benny Goodman playing clarinet*
- *Signs for Marshall Field, a store that began in Chicago*
- *A farmer using old-time equipment from McCormick, a company that started in Chicago*

eople from all over the world live in Illinois. Many people in Illinois work in **factories**. Some people make cars or tractors. Others print books. Some people farm. Abraham Lincoln lived in Illinois. He became the 16th president of the United States in 1861. A famous **clarinet** player named Benny Goodman lived in Illinois, too.

Chicago is the biggest city in Illinois. Almost three million people live there. Springfield is the capital of Illinois. The capital is where people in the **government** make decisions about laws for the state.

TOP, THEN LEFT TO RIGHT:
- *Downtown Chicago buildings at night*
- *Abraham Lincoln's house in Springfield*
- *The state capitol (main government building) in Springfield*
- *Chinatown, a part of Chicago where many people from China live*
- *A statue in Springfield over the place where Abraham Lincoln is buried*

16

Every year, many people visit a **skyscraper** in Chicago called the Willis Tower. Others go to Monks Mound. It is a big dirt structure that was built by American Indians. Illinois is full of interesting places!

TOP, THEN LEFT TO RIGHT:
- *Navy Pier, a shopping and entertainment center in Chicago*
- *Monks Mound, near the town of Collinsville*
- *A postcard from an Illinois state park*
- *Chicago's skyscrapers, including the tallest one, Willis Tower*

FACTS ABOUT ILLINOIS

First year as a state: *1818*

Population: *12,910,409*

Capital: *Springfield*

Biggest city: *Chicago*

Nickname: *The Prairie State*

State bird: *cardinal*

State flower: *violet*

State tree: *white oak*

A rocky Illinois area called
Garden of the Gods

GLOSSARY

American Indians—people who lived in America before white people arrived

clarinet—an instrument that is played by a person blowing into it, like a recorder

factories—places where people make things such as cars, toasters, or crayons

government—a group that makes laws for the people of a state or country

prairie—flat, treeless land covered by grasses

skyscraper—a very tall building

READ MORE

Fowler, Allan. *Illinois*. New York: Children's Press, 1999.

Wargin, Kathy-jo. *L Is for Lincoln: An Illinois Alphabet*. Chelsea, Mich.: Sleeping Bear Press, 2000.

LEARN MORE

Enchanted Learning: Illinois
http://www.enchantedlearning.com/usa/states/illinois/index.shtml
This site has Illinois facts, maps, and coloring pages.

Kids Konnect: Illinois
http://www.kidskonnect.com/content/view/177/27
This site lists facts about Illinois.

A view of Chicago and Lake Michigan

INDEX

American Indians 6, 19

animals 11, 12

attractions 19

cities 16

Goodman, Benny 15

jobs 15

Jolliet, Louis 6

land 9

Lincoln, Abraham 15

nickname 5, 20

people 6, 15, 16

plants 11, 12

rivers 9

weather 9

Cars being built in a factory in Illinois